WONDER
of the
WOODLANDS

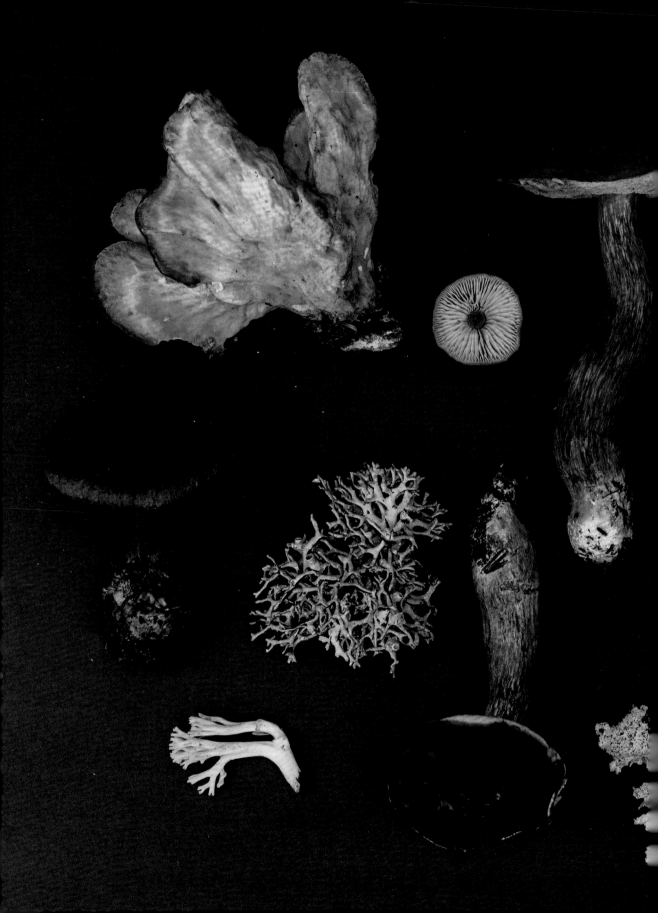

Wonder of the
WOODLANDS

The Art of Seeing and
Creating with Nature

FRANÇOISE WEEKS

with *Julie Michaels*

Photographs by Theresa Bear

Clarkson Potter / Publishers
New York

*I dedicate this book to my parents,
Louise and Georges De Wilder,
who instilled the love and respect for
Nature in their children from
a very early age*

Contents

Introduction

---

*I went to the woods because
I wished to live deliberately.*

— HENRY DAVID THOREAU

ere is the beauty of walking deep into the woods: you see small moments
with great clarity. This is particularly true when I spend the day foraging
in the forests of the Columbia Gorge or Mt. Hood. When I forage, I
do so on private land and always with permission. I have no destination in mind;
rather, I am on a treasure hunt. I might look for a grove of Douglas fir, beneath
which cherished chanterelles sprout. Or I might search the forest floor, looking
for dead limbs decorated in gray-green lichen.

Whatever the path, this walk is a visual adventure. I am looking for the odd
twist in a leaf, a branch still bearing its acorns, a mushroom sneaking its head out
from under softened moss. Each is a design element, something I might use as
inspiration for a forest-themed still life that will grace my dinner table or decorate
a quiet corner.

In the past decade, I have fallen in love with old-growth woodlands that
renew themselves by shedding old limbs and shading rocky trails with moss and
fern. These are woods untended by humans, where the process of birth, death,
and renewal follows the seasons. I have always been a woods-walker, but since
I began gathering bits of the forest to create one-of-a-kind arrangements, I
have found myself walking more deliberately. Each forest excursion becomes an
experience in itself, when time stops and Nature takes over.

Many of you will know what I am talking about. Especially during the hard days of the Covid-19 pandemic, people needed respite from their isolation, a sense of life continuing. That's why so many of us wandered outdoors. Many took a page from the Japanese tradition of *Shinrin-Yoku*, or "forest bathing." It's the practice of immersing yourself in Nature in a mindful way, using your senses to relieve anxiety and lower stress.

"In every walk with Nature, one receives far more than he seeks," wrote environmentalist John Muir. That's how I feel when the sun slants through trees on a late-spring afternoon and I spy a fragile blossom or discover a fledging nest. I am well-nourished by these forest walks, harvesting peace and tranquility as well as inspiration for my woodland projects.

MY WOODLAND JOURNEY

I grew up in Belgium, an active child, with parents who were avid Nature lovers. From the time I was six to age ten, we would spend a month each summer hiking in the Swiss Alps. Every year, my parents chose a village in a different region, each one storybook beautiful, with bright flowers cascading from tidy balconies.

In the evening, my father pored over maps of hiking trails, choosing one for the next day that promised magnificent views. My mother packed our lunches, and we would be off with the morning light, often hiking above the timberline. We climbed high enough to see whole valleys from our rocky purchase, pausing for photos in front of melting glaciers. Our visual appetite sated, my family would descend to a patch of forest green, where we relaxed during long lunch breaks. Often, my siblings and I wandered into the woods, found an unusual piece of bark, draped it in moss, and added a collection of wildflowers, proudly presenting the final arrangement to our mother.

Fast-forward forty-five years. I was married, living in Portland, Oregon, and—still smitten by Nature—earning my living as a successful floral designer. I casually mentioned this alpine memory to a photographer and art director,

while we were shooting photos for a book proposal. They suggested I create one of my woodland pieces for the photo shoot. Though I doubted they would use it, I found a lichen-covered log and decorated it with curly kiwi vine, a selection of seedpods, foliage from my garden, some store-bought succulents, and a variety of acorns. The resulting photographs were beautiful. Two months later, a bride—her fiancé's name was *Woods*—asked me to create a series of log motifs as table decorations for her wedding.

That was my woodland journey. One wedding assignment led to another and my work was being published in national and international magazines. I began creating unique still lifes for special events. I began teaching woodland design workshops and even developed an online course.

However, you don't have to live in the woodlands to make a woodland arrangement. In fact, most of the materials I use are from nurseries, flower markets, craft stores, and grocery stores. This book is the next step in showing people how they can gather inspiration from Nature to construct their own artful arrangements. Pay attention to the beauty found on your own walks in the woods—a log, tiny pinecones, a handful of young acorns, wild rose hips, or shapely seedpods. No one's inspiration will be the same; it depends on the seasons and where you live. Whatever the elements, the goal is to create a still life that captures a moment in Nature.

I've divided this book into chapters, each one illuminating a common building block in my arrangements, and each suggesting simple projects with steps to follow as well as many other projects that may inspire you. Since bark, logs, and branches form the backbone of my designs, I begin there, followed by chapters on mosses, mushrooms, acorns, lichens, and ferns.

I've included a list of tools and some instructions for how to make unique arrangements. But my primary goal is to teach you to see the artistry contained in any natural landscapes—be it ferns reaching up from the forest floor or acorns scattered through moss. I want you to see with a new pair of eyes.

HOW I SEE

As a floral designer, I had always focused on flowers, my gaze drawn to the perfect blossom. When I switched my focus to woodland design, I started to look at everything in the garden and in Nature from a different perspective. I paid more attention to the beautiful foliage of annuals, perennials, herbs, ground covers, and vines, incorporating them all into my designs. Checking for interesting seedpods of any plant became a new focus. Sometimes the beauty of a bud in my garden would catch my eye and I would snip this newly found treasure well before its bloom.

Rather than weed out the invasive wild strawberries that wandered among my sedum, I would harvest them to add whimsy to an arrangement. When pruning trees or shrubs, I would carefully gauge how usable the pieces would be in building a structure. I'd see a hollowed-out stump and wonder how I could repurpose it as a moss-covered "container." I memorized which trees grew where in my neighborhood, so I knew where to collect acorns and other seedpods when they dropped to the sidewalk. I'd seek out golden ginkgo leaves and other vibrant foliage while walking to the supermarket. My new eyes began to see beauty in the curling bark of a birch tree or the spore-laden bend of an autumn fern.

Gone are the days of hiking fast through the woods; now I wander with my eyes on the forest floor. During these stop-and-start rambles, I will gather the many varieties of pinecones, acorns, and lichens that I use in my still life arrangements. But I am a careful forager. Though I hike for inspiration on public land, I do most of my collecting in woods that are privately owned and where I have the owner's permission.

I am blessed to live in a city of parks and a state known for its dramatic coastline and farmlike country lanes. When I walk along Pacific beaches, my eyes are drawn to driftwood that I gather where it's allowed and use it in my work. I look, too, for seaweed that I soak, shape, dry, and weave into arrangements. Once you begin to spy items for your own forest still lifes, you'll find that every walk is an opportunity to find inspiration.

How I Build
an Arrangement

I work intuitively, surrounded by the many pieces of wood and bark I have collected over the years. I always know the purpose of my design, be it a centerpiece, a wreath, or even a necklace, but I have no detailed plans. Rather, the materials I have on hand will dictate the evolution of my design.

Sometimes a log thick with lichen will sit in my studio for years until inspiration strikes. If I'm looking for a vertical form, I might fasten on a second piece of bark to add height. Next, I glue on sheets of moss, which act as a base for the dried seedpods, cones, and berries that I glue into crevices and corners.

I follow my instincts, pairing slim twigs with circular mushrooms, blueberries with brown grasses. Though succulents are hardly a forest crop, they make their way into many arrangements because I find their shapes so pleasing: burro's tail, hedgehog aloe, tiny cactus—all gathered at my local garden center. You'll find that these add movement and color to a forest still life.

When you include fragile flowers in your pieces, make sure their stems are slipped into water-soaked AgraWool (see Tools, page 28), which provides hydration. With their stems hidden in lichen, the flowers look like they are emerging from the log.

Remember to save reusable food containers and inexpensive pots to use in smaller arrangements. If you cover them by gluing on bark or foliage, they become part of the design. Next, place a ball of crumpled chicken wire or AgraWool in which to hold branches and flowers, adding water so they remain fresh.

How much staying power do these projects have? That depends on their ingredients. If you build a wreath out of grapevine, lichen, pinecones, seedpods, and other dried materials, it can hang on the wall for months. If you use more fragile elements in a centerpiece, like flowering vines and other blossoms, make sure each living feature has access to a water source. These can last anywhere from five to seven days.

It's also possible to extend the life of an arrangement by replacing the more fragile bits as they dry out. For example, fresh ferns may wilt after a few days, but it's just a few steps out my back door to gather new ones. In fact, you can use the base of your dried centerpiece over and over again by adding new and different fresh elements. If you find a cache of wild strawberries or a pot of just-blooming crocuses, these can be tucked into an arrangement and give it a whole new look.

SOURCING MATERIALS

The beauty of the forest is that it's always changing, and so do my designs—in fall, I incorporate red rose hips and elderberries, and in spring, tiny green berries. Dried grasses, some with dramatic seed heads, are abundant. When you ramble, notice the seedpod, the curve of a fallen branch, or the peeling bark of a river birch.

Although I look to the forest for inspiration, I source most of my materials from the flower markets, nurseries, and grocery stores. You can make a woodland arrangement even if you don't live near a forest. It is very important to be respectful of Nature. I forage for ideas more than materials. I also often don't have time to forage for all the materials I need for a workshop or design project. So when it's time to create an arrangement, I use this way of seeing at the supermarket, the garden center, and the craft store. As much as I love using mushrooms harvested in the wild, most of the specimens in my arrangements come from a simpler source: the supermarket. You can find oyster, shiitake, cremini, or portobello mushrooms in many local markets. Once

dried, these mushrooms can become part of a larger arrangement or they can be displayed solo in a glass cloche. You can also do the same for adding berries to an arrangement. I frequently use succulents in my work, tiny plants not native to the forest, that I find in abundance at the flower market. I'm also drawn to the foliage of houseplants: begonias, the tiny offspring of a spider plant, or any bicolored leaf. You can purchase these plants from a garden center as you need them or raise your own. These are common plantings in a woodland garden, providing splashes of color when you pull them out of their pots—roots and all—and sink them into a carpet of moss. Dried grasses, ferns, and seasonal blossoms are readily available at a local flower shop. For more unusual materials such as blooming branches, moss, bark, or wooden disks, you can explore your local flower market or craft stores to find the materials you need. I am lucky to know several vendors at the Portland Flower Market who have permits to forage sustainably in the woods. It is a gift to have access to their selection of pinecones, catkins, seedpods, and foliage. Since moss is a living part of the forest, I seldom harvest my own. I'd rather purchase sheets of this greenery that have been responsibly cultivated.

Finally, there's my own garden, and gardens of friends, where I watch for hellebores to mature into seedpods. I wait until peonies set seed and gather their picturesque crowns, doing the same for nigella, dill, and anything else that captures my fancy. All make their way via my glue gun into my arrangements. Once you adopt the eyes of a woods-walker, you can ignore floral bouquets to discover a variety of hardy additions to your forest still lifes without disturbing Nature.

SEASONALITY

There's always something new to notice in the forest, which means there's always something new to inspire my woodland creations. In spring, before there are leaves on the trees, light illuminates previously dark corners and, miraculously, flowers appear. My joy during these early days is searching for spring ephemerals—short-lived woodland blossoms like trillium, trout lily, hepatica, and bloodroot. I never pick these precious flowers; they are not hardy and would never last in an arrangement. But they inspire me to visit my garden, where I harvest pink and purple hellebores, yellow witch hazel, burgundy fritillaria, and various shades and species of tulips. You can also use blossoms from the supermarket and garden center: alstroemeria, lilies, jade plants, tiny roses, or begonia leaves. Or choose pots of just-blooming bulbs—mini-daffodils, grape hyacinths, or tiny irises. All these and other similar greenery when hydrated in AgraWool (see Tools, page 28) or in a small water tube covered with moss or bark can reproduce the beauty you discover on the forest floor.

Many lichen-covered limbs are blown to the ground by winter storms and can easily be gathered from the sidewalk or in the backyard. Early rains have also fed beds of green moss, some of which I harvest, but only on property that is privately owned. You can find both fiddlehead ferns and moss at the market during spring and use them in your creations without taking anything from the forest.

In summer, the Pacific Northwest explodes with sunshine and I find myself drawn to the sea, trousers rolled up and always on the lookout for a stylish bit of driftwood. Oregon has an abundance of berries: blackberry, elderberry, blueberry, huckleberry, cranberry, and grapes all grow wild here. At the flower market early in the season, you can often find green, still unripe varieties that will last longer in your still lifes. And look to garden centers to find versions of in-season blooms and greenery that can be used to enhance your arrangements.

Fall is the season for mushroom hunting. I like to do my foraging with a good friend who knows more than I do about the thousands of varieties of mushrooms in this region. But even I can spot the orange-yellow funnels of the chanterelle or the broad, shiny caps of the spongy boletus, which is called

porcini in the supermarket. And the supermarket is often the best place to find mushrooms for drying and using in arrangements throughout the year. If you're lucky enough to live in a city or town with an abundance of oak trees or other nut-bearing trees, keep your eyes on the sidewalks during the fall. You'll be able to gather lots of dropped nuts that would otherwise be smashed under people's feet. Once dry, the nuts and seedpods can make their way into your arrangements.

Winter makes its own offering of red winterberries and holly. On warmer days, you can search the sidewalk for the papery bark of white birch trees that shed their older skin in this dark season. Because these birches can photosynthesize through bark, shedding their older skin allows these trees to manufacture carbohydrates, feeding the tree even before it leafs out. You can save the birch bark and glue it onto containers so even your receptacles look like part of the forest landscape. And if you can't find birch bark near your home, it's easy to find at craft stores along with birch disks that you can use as the base of arrangements.

COLOR, TEXTURE, MOVEMENT

No temperate forest is known for its radiant colors. Instead, my Oregon woods provide subtle contrasts: the grays, greens, and browns of the forest floor; the cinnamon cap of a quiet mushroom; or the scented berries of the blue juniper. If your goal is to re-create a forest scene—with acorns, pinecones, or bark—these subtle colors will be your palette.

Moss is the emerald addition that will illuminate quieter colors. Think of any dark forest path and recall that moss is a constant on most woodland hikes. Wherever there is moisture, these green cushions flourish, breaking down soil or growing on downed trees. Just as moss lights up the forest, it can form the base of your arrangements, adding contrast and drama.

What the forest lacks in vibrant color, it makes up for in intricate texture. I am amazed at the way Nature engineers the overlapping petals of a pinecone, the beret caps of acorns, or the swordlike leaves of ostrich ferns. Think about birch bark; its curling paper-white sheets add another rough surface to your designs.

A lichen-covered branch provides even more texture, with its gnarled bends and gray-green growths. Any woodland scene you build will rely on the juxtaposition of these textures.

Finally, you'll want to emphasize movement. Look for discarded branches that bend toward the sun or fiddleheads that are ready to unfurl. It is the rare still life that doesn't include a wandering vine, circles of dried seaweed, or curling bark. All these additions draw the eye through a piece, linking each element to its neighbor.

Once you understand the interplay of these three elements—color, texture, and movement—you can use them to capture a moment in Nature. None of us can reproduce the grandeur of a woodland scene in all its majesty, but by quoting its most memorable features, we can make arrangements that echo its impact.

Respecting and
Appreciating Nature

"I took a walk in the woods and came out taller than the trees," wrote Henry David Thoreau; I know what he meant. I do not want to take anything from the forest that will endanger it. We've taken too much already. I urge you to be careful in what you collect. Your best materials will be found on the forest floor, mostly dry elements that can last a long time in any arrangement, but be mindful about how much you take and how often you take from the same spots. Make sure you leave enough for the forest to continue about its business. Even better, consider leaving everything as you find it in forest spaces and forage instead on city sidewalks or in your own backyard, then supplement your finds with materials from the supermarket, garden center, flower market, and craft store.

In looking to this book for inspiration, each of you will have access to a different supply of materials. Some of you live in the country and can harvest ingredients on private woodland acres. (Be sure to ask for permission!) Urban foragers will be surprised at how much material they can find in any sizable city park. I do much of my foraging on morning walks with my border collie, Dory. Just walk with your eyes down and carry a large basket or shopping bag. I'm always coming home with dead limbs dislodged by a storm, pinecones, and all manner of other castoffs.

Please know that this kind of forest-inspired design is not flower arranging. Much as I love a vase full of beautiful blossoms, flowers are short-lived and, therefore, must be constantly replaced. The elements that go into many of my still lifes are recyclable. Since I do this work for a living and teach dozens of classes a year, I am an avid collector of ingredients. But if your goal is one centerpiece or six, you can work from a small collection of items again and again. The wooden bases you choose can be used repeatedly; so, too, can your lichen-encrusted branches. Keep a moss-covered log in your garage between arrangements and it will hold its color for months. Ditto acorns and pinecones. In fact, you can make a single arrangement using these ingredients and add and subtract shorter-lived elements as the seasons change. Add ferns in spring, mushrooms in fall, flowers until frost.

Woods-walking is mostly about foraging for ideas. I encourage you to focus on the small moments where Nature is the designer. Watch how she balances color, shape, and texture, and wonder at her evolutionary talent.

Use the natural world as inspiration. Gather your forest finds together with elements you've collected from the garden center or supermarket and make your own arrangements. There is no right or wrong to these creations. They are simply a combination of what you've learned by studying Nature balanced with your own creative vision. In the end, we all have the same goal: to make something beautiful.

TOOLS

Building an arrangement requires more than just a vase for holding flowers. Most of my pieces need some kind of structural support, whether that's a base or a frame on which to build. You'll also need different materials for attaching items to the support, ways to provide hydration when needed, and tools for cutting branches to the right size for your arrangements. To create the wild and delicate pieces seen in this book, here are some specific tools that will help. (If you're looking for tips on foraging respectfully for materials, see Notes on Foraging on page 231.)

AGRAWOOL

These biodegradable blocks are made from thin layers of mineral basalt and sucrose (usually cane or beet sugar), which are compressed into sheets and formed into bricks that you can cut to fit a vase or container. AgraWool has replaced the petrochemical-based foam that once was a standard for designers. When soaked in water, the wool can anchor delicate stems and provide steady hydration.

CHICKEN WIRE

When designing woodland arrangements in an opaque vase, I crumple some chicken wire in the container to anchor branches.

CLIPPERS

I use Felco #6 clippers since I have small hands. I use #4 clippers for thicker branches.

CONTAINERS

I save reusable food containers, inexpensive pottery, or glass vases that I cover with paper-thin bark, moss, or foliage, so they become part of the design. I sometimes use a tray with a half-inch lip onto which I glue large leaves. This lets me design in such a way that the container becomes invisible.

DRILL AND DRILL BIT

Sometimes it's necessary to attach one section of log or bark to another. Once you drill holes, you can attach the sections using screws or zip ties.

18-GAUGE WIRE

When I use succulents in designs with AgraWool, I create a "stem" for the cut succulent with wire. Cut a 3-inch piece of wire, dip the end in floral adhesive glue, and push it about 1 inch into the succulent.

FLORAL ADHESIVE GLUE

You can use this glue to attach any and all decorative elements, but it is essential whenever you are attaching living elements that still contain some water—like leaves to moss, succulents to wood, foliage to containers, or sheet moss to logs. There are several brands available, but I prefer Oasis.

HOT-GLUE GUN AND GLUE STICKS

These can be found in any craft store and are essential for gluing dried materials (seedpods, acorns, mushrooms, moss, lichen, etc.) to bark or wood. Many, including myself, prefer the ease of a hot-glue gun for attaching moss, acorns, seedpods, and other elements/materials.

DRIED SHEET MOSS

When designing on wood or bark, begin by gluing on a bit of moss first, then decorate with other elements. Sheet moss is often used as a base for my woodland frames. Dried sheet moss can be found at craft stores.

WATERPROOF TAPE

You can use this to create a grid at the mouth of a wide vase or to secure AgraWool to very low containers.

ZIP TIES

These are helpful in tying pieces of bark or branches together or fastening them to a supporting structure. You could attach the logs with screws, but I generally use zip ties.

1.

BARK, LOGS & BRANCHES

*Trees are poems that the earth
writes upon the sky.*
— KAHLIL GIBRAN

I was hiking in the woods with a friend one day and came across an impressive grove of oak trees, their dappled bark weathered into freckles of contrasting colors—browns, reds, and grays. Add a shaft of afternoon sunlight and you can understand the impact: I was transfixed. To me, that extraordinary contrast evoked the brushstrokes of a pointillist painting. Only Nature had done it better than Seurat.

Trees like this are the building blocks for any forest creation. At the flower market, I purchase stumps and bark. What should you look for? Texture—the feathery curls of paper-thin birch bark; depth—the hollow stump of a maple tree; and crenellation—the nooks and crannies of aging cedars. Search for ones sheathed in lichen and moss, or twisted into interesting shapes. Red and white oaks, Pacific madrone, eucalyptus, and birch are all on my list. Look to conifers for their generous supply of pinecones. Douglas fir, Sitka spruce, western hemlock: all have distinctive-looking cones in varying shapes and sizes. Most drop their cones from September through December; and you can often buy beautiful specimens at a flower market.

I buy my most dramatic logs to serve as the superstructure for my woodland still lifes. They are the base that holds moss and lichen, mushrooms, acorns, and seedpods. The more dramatic the base, the more likely my creation will be a showstopper.

When friends spy a knotty log in their garden, they'll bring it to my home, where it will join a chaotic woodpile in the backyard. Limbs and logs are stacked up in my workroom, waiting to be discovered for just the right arrangement.

You should look for wood that has been buffeted by the elements and scoured by the wind and rain. You might be inspired by a host of shelf mushrooms climbing up a limb, or like the way a narrow branch curves and twists. Our job is to take Nature's most dramatic toss-offs and make them into stars.

Think about recycling your favorite logs and branches. If I'm making a table arrangement for a wedding, for example, I'll invite the family to keep the decorated log for a week or two, until it dries out. But once the show has stopped, I'll reclaim the log for a future project.

I also have my favorite branches. One beauty is a circular branch that looks like the circumference of a giant tambourine. I purchased it from a forager at the Portland Flower Market who'd found it after a forest fire, when the branch had curved in the inferno (see page 192).

Look for wood that has been buffeted by the elements and scoured by the wind and rain.

When I create a table centerpiece, I'll often start with a horizontal log, preferably one that is punctuated with lichen. Using my glue gun, I might add some height with a magnolia branch heavy with buds. Mushrooms, succulents, or twining ivy will come next.

If you want to create a taller structure, drill holes in a vertical piece of wood, then attach the wood with zip ties to a more horizontal base. Since the aim is to re-create a forest moment, you might then glue on moss and bits of lichen, followed by acorns and pinecones. Many unusual, nonlocal varieties are sent to me by former students.

Like the Dutch masters who painted abundant floral still lifes, many with flowers that never bloomed at the same time, we are not aiming for reality. Rather, our goal is to imitate Nature by enhancing the visual experience.

How I See . . .
BARK

It's the rare woods-walker who can't tell the difference between a maple leaf and an oak leaf. We pride ourselves on reading the forest canopy in spring and summer. But what about winter when the trees are bare of leaves? It's then we look for a second time at the always constant bark. Woody trunks can range from shaggy hickory to shedding birch, each with its own distinctive pattern. Cracks in bark are a great habitat for insects and a feedlot for birds. When a tree dies, its bark serves a second life as home to lichens, mosses, and ferns. It's this older, creviced bark that I find most appealing for my arrangements. It has the character of age.

Tips for Making
A BARK TROUGH

The container pictured below looks like it's made from a hollowed-out birch tree. It's actually a plastic container covered in this useful "forest paper." I much prefer using odd containers like this than employing traditional vases for my work. I want the viewer to think they've stumbled upon a tiny bit of the forest floor, just greening into spring.

Using a glue gun, attach the bark to the outside of the plastic container, adding bits of lichen to cover any awkward seams. If you line these containers with moss, you can add small fruits and/or vegetables for a summer tablescape. Here, I placed small stones at the bottom of the container for drainage. Then I used potted plants, like spring violas, daffodils, or muscari, removing them from their pots and inserting them into the trough. You can also fill the container with some well-watered AgraWool and design a lovely arrangement with cut flowers and textures. Use moss or lichen to drape over the edges of the trough. You can use the trough repeatedly by simply replacing the flowers with other seasonal blossoms or succulents.

Bring It Home

BOTANICAL BOOKENDS -
(*previous pages*) An old desk boasts
cubbies filled with mushrooms and
birch logs. (*right*) Mason jars store
mushrooms and dried flowers.
(*far right*) A wood base is decorated
in moss, mushrooms, and lichen.

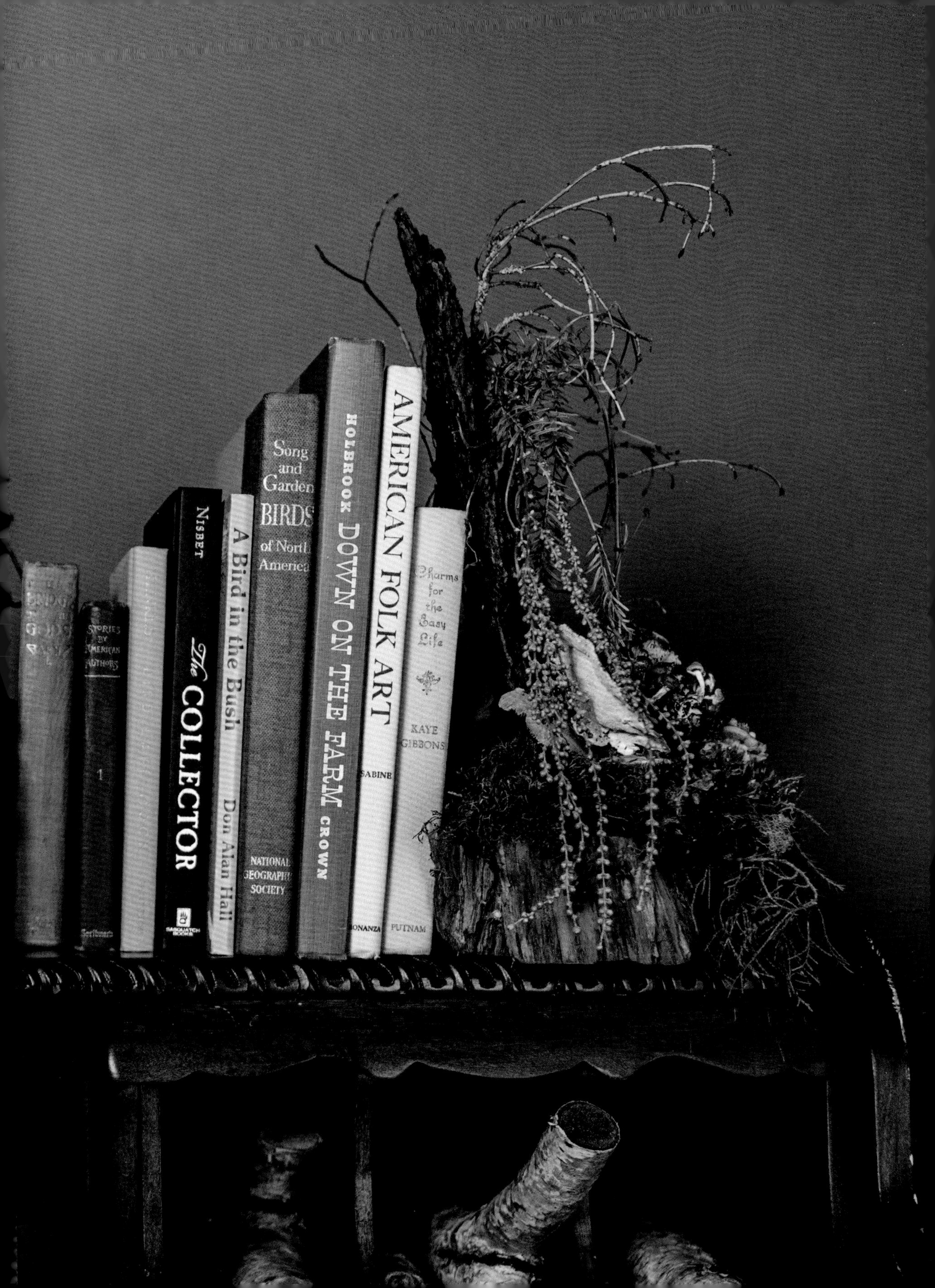
Stories by American Authors
Scribners
Nisbet
The Collector
Sasquatch Books
A Bird in the Bush
Don Alan Hall
Song and Garden Birds of North America
National Geographic Society
Holbrook
Down on the Farm
Crown
American Folk Art
Sabine
Bonanza
Charms for the Easy Life
Kaye Gibbons
Putnam

FOREST BASKET - Here's an easy decoration for the guest bedroom: Gather some birch limbs—these have the added beauty of green lichen attached to some boughs—and place them in a tall container. I like using wicker because it reinforces the natural element, and you can hide a vase filled with water inside the basket. Add branches of just-blooming forsythia, a magnolia limb heavy with buds, and whatever else piques your fancy.

PANSY AND BIRCH WALL HANGING - This wall hanging (also see on page 44) was fashioned with strips of birch bark that were glued onto a wooden two-by-four. To achieve this look, cut strips of birch bark (1" × 12"), soak them in water, bend them around a vase, let them dry, and then hot-glue them onto the 2 × 4. Pansies were harvested from the garden, treated in a hydration chamber for 24 hours, then cold-glued onto the bark along with *Pieris* flowers and *Pieris* seedpods.

HOW TO MAKE A HYDRATION CHAMBER - Some flowers, like these pansies, can last for 24 hours without a water source if they are conditioned. I do this by placing the flowers into a lidded, plastic container with some damp paper towels. Put the container in the refrigerator for 24 hours, removing the flowers just before you arrange them.

LOG MANTEL DECORATION - This arrangement is all about the funky, lichen-encrusted log that forms the base. Logs like this have so many indentations that they are perfect for holding all manner of materials. Start by affixing moss with floral glue. Once this dries, glue on seedpods, branches, and acorns. Using more floral glue for still-living elements, I added succulents, beargrass, and ferns.

BARK FRAME *(opposite)* - Using a square wire frame as a base, I glue on curled pieces of eucalyptus bark gathered from a neighborhood sidewalk. You might use lichen-covered twigs or peeling birch branches instead. Sometimes, less is more. Glue a variety of succulents, mushrooms, acorns, poppy seedpods, screwbean mesquite, and pinecones into the bottom corners of the frame, leaving much of the frame's flaky wooden texture exposed.

PINECONE CHANDELIER - Gather
a variety of lichen–covered branches
and glue them together into a "bird's
nest." You can add acorns or other forest
ephemera as you please. Attach pinecones
to clear fishing line and hang them from
the nest, creating a forest chandelier.
Hang one or two above your dining table,
where they will last for months.

CORK CONTAINER – I like making my own containers. Two reasons: it's less expensive to fashion my own container around a plastic pot than to purchase something more costly; it also means I can use natural elements to make the container part of my design. Here, I purchased sheets of cork in a craft store, tore them into irregular shapes, and glued the pieces onto a plastic pot. This one is filled with hellebores and maidenhair ferns, but you can add any elements to the mix.

BARK STANDS FOR STILL LIFE –
You can use various forest elements
to create still lifes in any quiet corner.
Here, I combined birch logs of varying
heights with a base of chartreuse
lichen. Two blooming purple hyacinths
explode with color, their exposed
roots adding to the drama. You can
plunge the hyacinth roots in water each
evening, which will keep the bulbs
fresh for a week.

LOG AND FERN TABLESCAPE –
This table centerpiece relies on the natural drama of a beautifully aged log. It draws the eye to explore the various shapes of shelf fungi, punctuated by bits of lichen. You can contrast all that brown and gray by adding small vases to your table, each holding a different type of fern. Another fern rests on the table napkin, carrying the Nature theme forward. The log will keep for months; you can replace the ferns with tiny flowers or other greenery.

WOODEN CRADLE - This striking wooden "cradle" was found on a forest ramble. It's recycled frequently to hold all manner of forest flotsam. Here, it rests on a moss base and holds a dramatic succulent paired with green cotinus flowers and purple sweet peas. The cotinus and pea flowers will wither without water, but their slow wilting is part of the natural process.

2.

MOSS

---

*All overgrown with azure moss
and flowers so sweet.*
— PERCY BYSSHE SHELLEY

O regon is known for its coastal fog. That's not so nice for tourists who long for ocean views, but for those of us in search of moss and lichen, damp weather is the engine that builds our green forests.

At least once a year, I travel to Cape Meares, just west of Portland, to enjoy the picturesque driftwood and hike through the rainforest that hugs the coast. The trees here literally drip with moss. It also covers rocks, old foundations, and ruined structures—any surface where spores can lodge and grow. Rough winds play havoc with the older timbers, leaving the forest floor scattered with broken limbs enveloped in green.

Moss is one of Nature's great inventions. On the Oregon coast, numerous varieties soak up rainfall, maintain moisture in the soil below, and keep conditions humid so trees can thrive. These ancient plants—they've been discovered on fossils dating back more than 450 million years—occur on every continent and in every ecosystem habitable by plants that use sunlight for energy. But these green pillows are not always abundant. Last year, when I visited New Jersey to lead a woodlands workshop, my hosts took me hiking in the state forest. The rocks and trees seemed scrubbed clean. No green moss covered their limbs; the forest floor was brown with decaying leaves, but except for a shaded boulder here and there, there was precious little moss. I realized how different these woods are from the ones back home.

Moss has been discovered on fossils dating back more than 450 million years.

Generally, moss doesn't damage trees. Since it doesn't have roots, the plant attaches via rhizoids, small hairlike structures that anchor to rocks, bark, or soil. In a particularly wet environment, they may bring down limbs just by growing too heavy. It's these broken limbs that provide inspiration for how I design with moss in my arrangements. That said, I generally buy moss from licensed vendors in the flower market. Craft stores sell moss by the bag, or you can order it online.

When you begin work on a new arrangement, your first task after establishing a base should be to apply a sheet of moss to the wood with quick-drying floral adhesive. This establishes a "bed" for the decorations that come after, which can be anchored into the moss using a hot-glue gun. You can glue nuts and acorns into one nook, mushrooms into a nearby cranny. The goal is to create a small version of the forest floor, where soft moss colonizes barren soil and Nature is busy regreening the earth.

HOW TO WORK WITH MOSS

In Nature, moss is generally found in damp spots, and it loves to soak up water. If you store moss in a lidded plastic container, it will hold moisture longer. Once you glue moss into an arrangement, spray it with water once a week to keep it looking fresh.

It's best to buy large amounts of moss from a reputable seller.

How I See . . .
MOSS

Moss knits rock to earth. If you had
several decades to observe one forest
patch, you might even see its tiny
rhizomes turn rock into soil. The bright
green abundance of moss, whether
clinging to the north side of a tree or
crawling along a stone wall, always
delights me. Look closely and you'll see
the odd acorn or twisted leaf in a bed
of moss; touch it and discover Nature's
own pillow. I use moss to re-create that
sense of softness in the forest, using it to
embrace other elements and add texture.

Tips for Making
A FAIRY HOUSE

A fairy house is a bit of whimsy created out of natural elements. Whether you build it around a tree stump, like the one pictured here, or on a birch disk to mimic a natural shelter for an imaginary creature, building a fairy house is a delightful way to make a woodland arrangement that is playful as well as beautiful.

On a sunny afternoon, I took my baskets of dried forest elements and brought them to this stump to create something new. First, I used cold glue to attach moss, lichen, and larger seedpods to the trunk. Then I layered on hairy moss, perky mushrooms, acorns galore, and wacky seedpods—just the kind of home a forest elf would enjoy.

Bring It Home

GRAPE HYACINTH TROUGH –
Here's a wooden boat, captained by
grape hyacinths. This trough is in my
collection of containers and often used
for dinner parties. Again, my source is the
supermarket, where these blue caps appear
in early spring. Line your trough with
cling wrap before adding any plants. Buy
a few small containers of these hyacinths,
pull them from the pots and sink them
into the trough (you can leave a few white
roots dangling), cover with moss, and add
any seedpods that are scattered on the
sidewalk or in your backyard.

MOSS MINI MOMENT - Practice creating small moments in your home. Here, a sheet of leggy moss leans against two old books, complementing a Greek bust. The moss can be used again for another project.

MOSS CARPET - Talk about turning heads at your next cocktail party! As a bit of whimsy, this moss carpet was "planted" under a coffee table. I started by laying a piece of plastic on the floor to protect it. I added a crusty log or two and a variety of mosses, then glued lichens, ferns, and dried mushrooms onto the moss. The carpet was deep enough to disguise small pots of violets and pansies. Spray once a week with water to keep the arrangement fresh.

MOSS TABLESCAPE - An outdoor dinner table intersperses islands of moss with candles and even a mushroom under glass. The pièce de résistance is a lichened log decorated with ferns, shelf mushrooms, dried seaweed, and even a tiny cactus. Use cold floral glue for attaching the elements, and spray once a week with water to keep the arrangement perky.

MOSS TABLESCAPE, SIDE VIEW –
Another view of the dramatically arched
log that dominates the dinner table.
Dried bean pods dangle from a branch
that's been decorated with a "kitchen
sink" of forest detritus: acorns, berries,
seedpods, mushrooms, even a pair of
desiccated Venus flytraps. I collect many
of these dried elements throughout
the year, shopping through the flower
market, gathering and sorting my
collection into large baskets. Sitting
down to "dress" a log, I have plenty
of elements from which to choose.

MOSS CENTERPIECE - Even without any table settings, this dramatic decorated log provides a focal point. While the level of detail here is not vital to every project, the close-up shot on the facing page shows how much visual interest can be packed into any arrangement.

FRAMED FLOWERPOTS – These wooden tray/frames are sold at most hobby shops. They are perfect for building still life portraits you can hang on the wall. Start the "portrait" by using cold glue to attach moss to the base of the tray. Secure a piece of bark using a drill and zip ties to act as the base, then attached the flowerpots in the same way. Once those are secure, line the pots with plastic and add a little chicken wire and water. That will secure things and keep them hydrated. Then place purple hyacinths, or any other spring blossom, into the containers. You can decorate the portrait by gluing on branches or whatever else you fancy. I added hellebores secured in a water tube hidden in the moss. Spray once a week with water to keep the moss fresh.

FOREST APRON – This is a simple canvas apron that's become a forest backdrop. Start by hot-gluing and zip-tying picturesque pieces of bark to the bottom, then decorate with acorns, hellebores, bark mushrooms, moss, a bib of lichen, and a few checkerboard fritillaria, set into water tubes and hidden among the crowd.

BLOOMING SINK - Pink hellebores soak in a kitchen sink, their soil covered in moss. The windowsill holds three exposed muscari bulbs and a quartet of paler hellebores in a demitasse cup.

MOSSY MUSHROOM SEAT –
This versatile moss cushion can
also be on display on a plate
or birch round for an artful
centerpiece. All the mushrooms
were purchased at the local
supermarket. Glue a piece of moss
onto a tray or just a cardboard
pizza round. Then glue on the
mushrooms, adding the odd fern
here and there. When the party's
over, rescue the mushrooms
and reuse them.

3.

MUSH-
ROOMS

The mushroom is the elf of plants.
— EMILY DICKINSON

As a child, hiking in the woods with my parents, I was delighted to discover a colony of mushrooms peeking out from under fallen leaves. They seemed like little gnomes, appearing after a rainstorm, like a troupe of forest magicians.

I still enjoy foraging for fungi in places where it is permitted and delight in their descriptive common names: lion's mane, hedgehog, bear's tooth, black trumpet, morel, turkey-tail, lobster, and chicken of the woods, to name just a few. It's best to use the sturdiest of these to add a dramatic, earthy quality to your arrangements. Once dried, they last for weeks in a wreath or tablescape, surrounded by mosses, seedpods, succulents, nuts, and berries.

Except for our deserts, mushrooms are abundant in all parts of the United States. The Pacific Northwest boasts more than fifteen hundred varieties in rainbow hues of purple, red, and yellow. Since most fungi flourish in the damp, they usually appear with the rains of early spring and again in the fall. Their abundance—or lack thereof—depends on the weather. You should plan your outings a day or two after a hard rain, when mushrooms, in their many forms, pop up from the forest floor.

Most of the mushrooms in my arrangements come from a simpler source: the supermarket.

Since I am more romantic plant lover than mycologist, I gather mushrooms with a friend who is more familiar with the hundreds of species that flourish in my region. Although I can tell a golden chanterelle from a crenellated morel, it's best to rely on the experts, even if I have no intention of eating my harvest.

You don't need much equipment for mushroom hunting. Carry a wicker basket or a backpack for your finds, or maybe a mesh bag. Either way, spores can fall from the mushrooms you've picked and populate next season's crop. Use a curved mushroom knife (see photo on page 108) to make a clean cut without disturbing the belowground fungus. A soft narrow paintbrush will remove the dirt off your mushrooms without damaging their skins. And, of course, make sure you have the necessary permits or permission before taking anything from the forest.

It's easy to locate so-called bracket, or shelf, mushrooms. These are tough and woody in appearance and are normally found growing on tree trunks. They belong to the polypore family and are semicircular in shape. Usually, they sprout directly from a tree trunk, developing in old wounds or cracks on the bark.

Since these shelf fungi do a tree no favor, you should feel comfortable harvesting them to use in your still lifes (with permission, of course). If you discover a variety of shelf fungi on a collection of dead limbs, you can display them in groups, leaning the combo against a wall as if they were walking sticks gathered for a chat.

Since the mushrooms we collect are intended for still life arrangements, they need to be dried (see below). Unless properly dehydrated, they will rot and lose their shape. Along with those bracket mushrooms, you should seek out hardier varieties, which include some famous edibles: chanterelles, shiitakes, and the giant *Boletus edulus,* or porcini mushrooms, with a cap that looks like a leprechaun could sit on it. This last one dries so well that I can often keep it for many weeks, either in an arrangement or individually displayed.

As much as you may love searching out mushrooms in the wild, most of the mushrooms in my arrangements come from a simpler source: the supermarket. In recent years, many markets have moved beyond the solitary, pale button mushroom to offer multiple varieties on the grocery store shelves. When preparing for a workshop, or stymied by a rainy spell, I can find oyster, shiitake, cremini, porcini, and portobello mushrooms in many local markets.

HOW TO DRY MUSHROOMS

The easiest way to dry mushrooms is to arrange your finds on a paper towel without them touching, and let them sit for five to seven days to dry out. Another option is a food dehydrator. Set the heat at 125°F and wait three to four hours. Finally, you can turn on your oven to 100°F, spread the mushrooms out on a cookie sheet, and, with the oven door cracked open, check them after two to four hours.

FIND A RELIABLE GUIDE

You don't need much in the way of
equipment to find and pick mushrooms,
but it's always wise to educate yourself.
Look for a field guide to your particular
region; there are several series for the
Pacific Northwest, the Midwest, the
Southwest, and the Northeast. I also like
to carry an accordion-folded chart that
has photos of popular mushrooms on a
single laminated page. If you have access
to the internet on your walks, you can
download a mushroom identification
app. A favorite of mine is iNaturalist,
which not only lets you ID mushrooms,
but pinpoints where you found them
so you can return there year after year.
Even better is to find a reliable in-person
guide so that you can avoid picking
anything dangerous.

Mushroom picking for personal use
is often permitted on public land. At
Mount Rainier National Park, for
example, each visitor is allowed to pick
one gallon of an edible variety per day.
Professional harvesters must apply for
permits. You should check for foraging
rules that are posted on the websites
of many state or national parks before
you visit. Some require registration,
but you don't have to pay a fee. I never
harvest mushrooms from private property
without permission.

How I See . . .
MUSHROOMS

Since mushrooms do not contain chlorophyll, they cannot produce their own food using the process of photosynthesis. Instead, they rely on two sources of nourishment. First, you'll see decomposers, fungi that feast on rotting logs and other dying organic material. Second, you'll come across mushrooms growing at the base of a tree or another root system using a symbiotic relationship to share nutrients with their host.

When I compose a forest still life, I use this visual knowledge to snuggle my mushrooms into the elbow of a log or set them deep into a bed of moss, recreating their natural situation in the forest.

Tips for Making
A SPORE PRINT

Curious mycologists know that one way of identifying an unknown mushroom is to make a "spore print." These tiny seeds, hidden in a mushroom's gills, create a pattern when placed onto white paper or card stock. Seeing the color or size of the spore helps identify the species. I enjoy making spore prints because they are beautiful, another form of natural art. I might hang the prints on the wall above my desk, or even frame them for friends.

To make a print, remove the stalk from a fresh mushroom so only the cap remains. Place the mushroom on a piece of paper, gill side down. Place a bowl over the cap to keep it anchored and leave it overnight.

In the morning, remove the cap to discover the spores arrayed in a circular pattern. If you want to keep your prints and arrange them as wall art, simply spray with an art store fixative, the same way you'd preserve charcoal or pastel drawings.

Bring It Home

STILL-LIFE DISPLAY – A variety of dried mushrooms adorn this page. (*above*) A chanterelle. (*left*) Two large porcini mushrooms are held erect in a pin vase, creating the illusion that the mushrooms are growing straight up out of the desk.

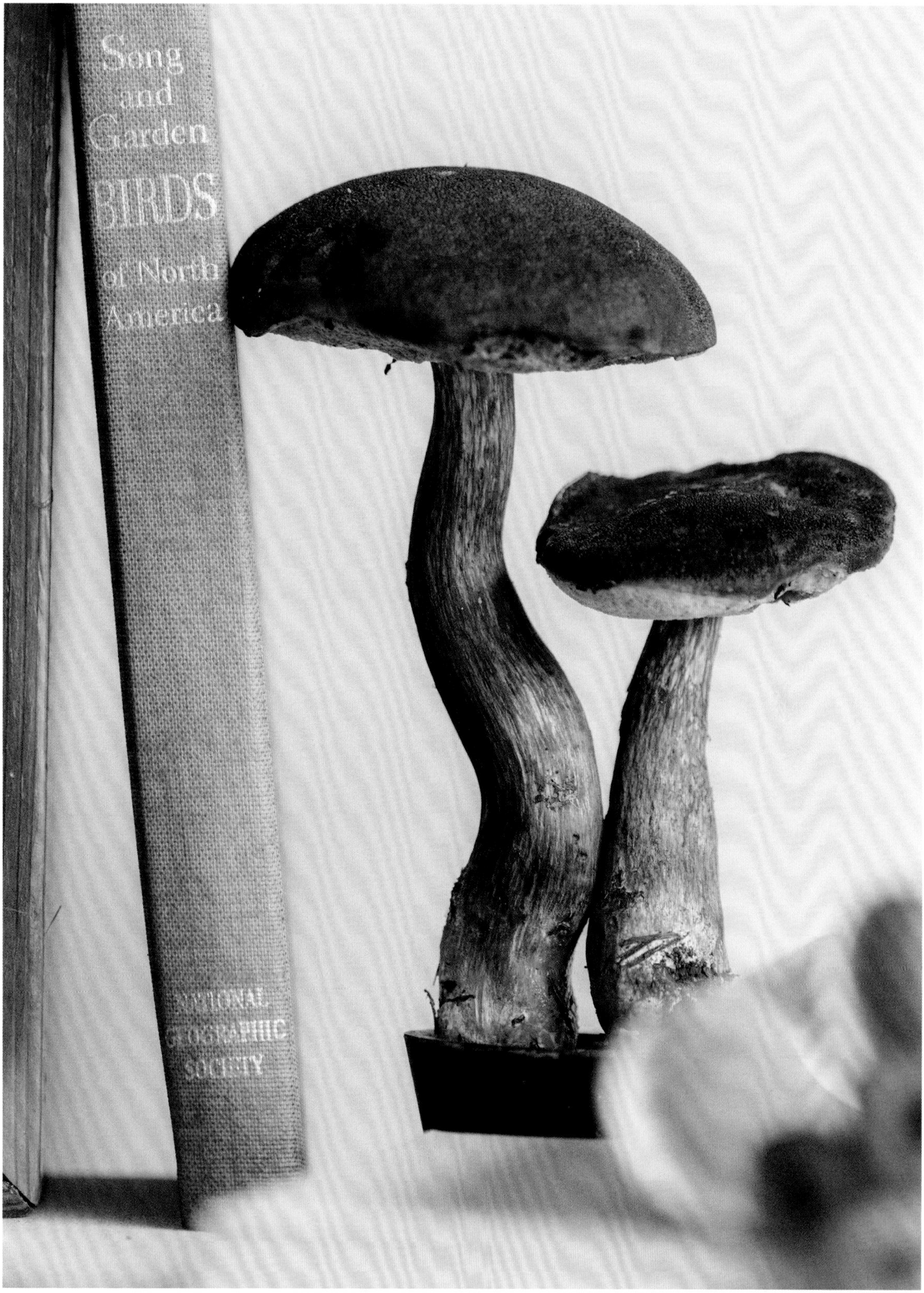
Song
and
Garden
BIRDS
of North
America

When foraging for mushrooms, always go with an expert who can
positively identify the mushrooms you find. If you aren't sure of a
mushroom's identity, it's best to leave the wild mushrooms where they
are and instead re-create their beauty with fungi from the grocery store
or farmer's market.

MUSHROOM TOWER –
Here's an example of using
two logs, one as a base, and
the other—attached to the base
with zip ties passed through
drilled holes—as a vertical element.
While I concentrate the mushroom
collection in the "lap" of the
display, I drape the tall log in
wisps of evergreen and young
branches, as if they were dancing
above the crowd.

MUSHROOM TOWER, CLOSE UP –
Here again, the mushrooms look exotic,
but most were picked from supermarket
shelves. They are held by a bracket
mushroom base that came from the
forest and are joined by a bevy of acorns,
poppy seedpods, and a dusting of gray-
green lichen.

MUSHROOM TREE ARRANGEMENT - A thick vine wrapped itself around this moss-encrusted tree and still embraces it. The two form the dramatic background for a tower of mushrooms. A wooden base with two tall dowels stabilizes the vine and the moss-covered bark. I glued sheet moss to that base and created a small garden of mushrooms, pieris foliage, a spider plant, and acorn caps. I added more branches of pieris, a variety of mushrooms, evergreen foliage, a branch of bracket mushrooms, and budding magnolia branches.

ENOKI MUSHROOM POT – This design begins with a plastic flowerpot with thin bark glued on. A curving branch covered in leathery shelf mushrooms adds drama. A "hat" of moss holds a ballet of tiny, dried enoki mushrooms.

BRACKET MUSHROOM BRANCH - Here, a white bracket mushroom, set in a hollow branch, provides the backdrop to a trio of dried mushrooms: chanterelle, enoki, and boletus. A variety of seedpods and a cascade of green ivy brings it all together.

SHELF DISPLAY – This arresting display starts with a large white shelf mushroom, placed in a hollow log base. Lichen, dried mushrooms, ivy, and a tiny spider plant rise gracefully from the shelf mushroom. The two seedpod "horns" sit on top, adding some movement. Oak leaves are also entwined with the taller ivy plant, adding a touch of gold to the greenery.

STILL-LIFE PAIR – The still life (*opposite*) boasts a base of birch bark shavings, paired with the green tops of a pieris bush. Layered above are more birch bark, acorn caps, black fungus, ferns, seedpods, and looping pieces of dried seaweed. (*below*) A glass vase holds cobaea vine, buds, and seedpods. A group of mushrooms and seedpods top it off.

STILL-LIFE PAIR, CLOSE UP – (*opposite*)
Pieris, seedpods of cobaea (cup-and-saucer vine),
and wispy lichen form the base. (*above*) Two
types of mushrooms add drama.

MUSHROOM WINDOW DISPLAY - This kitchen counter boasts two still lifes (details on pages 129–130) and a deftly woven lanyard of garlic and dried flowers hanging above the stove.

MUSHROOM BOWL - A collection of enoki and morel mushrooms is displayed in a "found" wooden bowl and embellished with pinecones, seedpods, and cotinus flowers.

WINDOW BOX – A rectangular stone tray, lined with ferns, holds an array of dried mushrooms, including enokis and morels, interspersed with acorns, lichens, and seedpods.

4.

ACORNS & SEEDPODS

The creation of a thousand forests is in one acorn.

— RALPH WALDO EMERSON

I am fortunate to live in a Portland neighborhood that cherishes its abundant tree canopy. While walking my dog, Dory, on a windy autumn day, I often hear the staccato of falling acorns—*Plonk! Bang! Dribble! Plonk!*—as we enter a nearby park. Acorns lie everywhere on the ground.

I always bring a bag on these excursions and, while Dory visits with her canine playmates, I'll collect acorns, seedpods, lichens, or whatever else has fallen to the pavement. Carried back to my studio and laid out to dry, this forest flotsam will eventually make its way into my arrangements. I find it particularly charming that I have gathered all this natural beauty within a few blocks of my own backyard.

Acorns are Nature's great invention: with their jaunty, crenellated caps and smooth green/brown seeds, they symbolize potential, since each one carries a great oak at its core. Our North American forests boast more than fifty-eight varieties of oak, and each produces its own style of acorn. These range from the massive, deeply fringed caps of the burr acorn, which looks more like a chestnut, to the smaller, more familiar nuts of the red and white oaks.

Here in Oregon, the white oak is most abundant. The Kalapuya and other Native American tribes cultivated the trees in open grasslands that they frequently burned so the oaks would grow tall and feed the elk and deer that sustained them. Since mature Oregon white oaks are fire-resistant, they would not be harmed by the low-intensity fires. Known as savannas, these oak forests are mostly gone, but enough of the trees remain to allow me a generous harvest.

I begin gathering acorns in the early summer when nuts are tiny and green on the bough. Wind and rain will strip whole branches from the trees, so much can be harvested from the ground, even in more urban settings. With leaves removed, these branches might appear as miniature trees in my arrangements.

My main harvest comes in the fall, from September through November, when a walk with my dog or in private woodlands rewards me with an abundance of fallen acorns. According to scientists at the University of California, Davis, only one in ten thousand acorns grows into a tree.

I generally use the acorns whole, attaching them to my superstructure with a glue gun. But you can also "decapitate" acorns and use just the bottoms. If the caps don't come off easily, just soak them in water for an hour and then separate. I use acorns in most of my work, but they always make an appearance in my woodland frames and wreaths.

Given that acorns are abundant in the Oregon woods, I don't have to stint on using them. They are not a material I save and recycle. I even receive gifts of unusual acorns from former workshop students who send me their local harvests.

Since oaks are the largest tree genus (*Quercus*) in the United States, you should be able to identify a local forest that can provide a fall harvest. Should you live in Idaho, Alaska, or Hawaii, where oak trees are not native, you can always order acorns online.

After acorns, seedpods are a constant favorite in my work. In my years as a floral designer, I was drawn to flowers in full bloom, eager to admire their perfection. But now I am much more fascinated by that final thrust of the plant to reproduce—the ingenious seedpod.

Since plants cannot travel to spread their genetic material, they have evolved by using sophisticated techniques to scatter their seeds. A burdock, for example, will attach itself to anything passing by, while a poppy requires only a brief shake to disperse hundreds of tiny black seeds around the garden.

The peony, when in bloom, is sheer glory in the garden. But if you watch its seed head through the season, you'll witness wedgelike pods that finally crack open to reveal shiny black or purple seeds. They seem positively prehistoric. Displayed amid mushrooms and lichen in a still life, they will surprise the viewer, who wonders what they are.

The most useful seedpods are those that dry well: abutilon, beech, cardiocrinum, eucalyptus, hellebore, honey locust, nicandra, nigella, peony, pieris, poppy, sweetgum, and wisteria. Some of these I raise myself, some I harvest from a friend's autumn garden. Some are sent to me by former students.

I also gather milkweed pods, when I can find them. Lupines and wisteria, both members of the pea family, also create remarkable pods.

Track down other more exotic pods—like lotus, palm, or acacia—at the flower market. Or they can be ordered online.

You can augment these sturdy seeds with other favorites that have less staying power. The berries of pieris, euonymus, and viburnum will collapse as they desiccate, but if you provide a water source in your arrangements, they will last for days. These and other berries can be easily sourced at flower markets as well.

Acorns and seedpods are constants in my work. Once they are dry, I can store the various types in baskets in my studio. When I begin work on a project, I surround myself with these containers—as if they were drawers full of odd-shaped nuts and bolts. Once I glue moss and lichen onto my base, I look for shapes that complement each other and—glue gun in hand—I begin building my piece, adding branches, tucking acorns into corners, or weaving dried vines up and through my work. As you create your own still lifes, your goal should be to capture a forest moment, one that is romanticized even as it echoes the natural world.

CHANGES IN ACORNS OVER TIME

One delight about acorns is how they change over time. You might begin with green acorns that will mature into shades of brown—from caramel to deep umber and dark chocolate. With time, the acorns might split or become wizened, but they will still carry an organic beauty. Each time you return to your acorns, they will add different things to your arrangement, depending on how old they are.

The most useful seedpods
are those that dry well.

How I See . . .
ACORNS

There's something so joyful about an
acorn. Walking in an oak grove, it's as if
the trees have decided to toss you tiny
presents, one more perfect than the next.
These are the most familiar nuts in our
woods, and when I see them scattered on
the ground or hanging from branches, I
feel Nature has done all the work. How
could anyone improve on these top–
hatted beauties?

Tips for Making
A SEEDPOD FRAME

A forest still life is a beautiful way to display your wild creations, and it offers something different from a more traditional table arrangement. Some of the projects in this book use prebought frames or boxes, like this one, but for others I construct the frame from lichen-encrusted branches and leave the center empty.

Wood-edged boxes, like the one shown here, are for sale in most craft stores. They make excellent containers for a forest still life you can hang on the wall.

Start by gathering your ingredients. (*opposite*) Here, I use moss, branches, seedpods, succulents, green raspberries, and a long winding vine. Arrange the grouping on a table, until the combinations look balanced.

Use hot glue to attach moss to the base. Once that dries, attach other elements with hot glue. Experiment with the smaller elements to see where they look best. Here there are some small branches, twining vines, succulents, seedpods, and a few baby acorns. Once you find a pleasing arrangement, glue them into place. Should you want to introduce flowers, simply secure them into water tubes you can sink into the moss.

Bring It Home

JEWELRY COLLECTION - Though most of my work is creating forest still lifes, I also hold workshops for designing jewelry inspired by Nature. (*above*) This necklace is strung with eucalyptus seedpods. At the front, I glued on pieces of birch bark, lichen, seedpods, and tiny acorns. (*opposite*) A dramatic pair of earrings with mushrooms, birch bark, lichen, and succulents hot-glued to the base. Both of these pieces have been modeled in fashion shows.

ACORN WREATH - Here's a dried wreath with all natural elements hot-glued onto a wire frame. You might call it a "kitchen sink" creation. In the course of a year, I collect a huge variety of seedpods, pinecones, acorns, and succulents. Students who've taken my courses often send me contributions from their own nearby forests or gardens. All of these materials go into a variety of baskets, until I save up enough pieces to take out my glue gun and compose this kind of magical wreath. I might glue on a few lichen-covered twigs to add dimension or add a few red eucalyptus flowers, but with a spritz from a water bottle every few weeks, this wreath can last for months, indoors or out.

OUTDOOR WALL HANGING – At the base of this wall hanging are intertwined ivy roots that no doubt killed the tree they were hugging. Using a hot-glue gun, I added dried calathea leaves, acorns, tillandsia, rhipsalis, string of pearls succulent, a spider plant, and lichen.

ACORN CHAIR - (*opposite*) A collection of "walking sticks" gathered after a severe windstorm. The birch limb, still trailing its leaves, complements the lichen- and mushroom-encrusted pair that bow out next to the acorn-studded stool. To add a bit of whimsy, I taped a colorful branch to the wall, adding another of fresh pine. (*above*) A close-up of the acorn stool, its seat cheerfully covered in acorns.

FOREST HAT - Two views of a straw hat, its crown covered in maple leaves, the brim a field of acorns, with a jaunty snip of pieris buds acting as a "feather." All this takes is a hot-glue gun, and patience.

FOREST FRAME - Another wooden tray/frame holds this forest "painting" (see page 145 for ideas of how to re-create a similar arrangement). Start by gluing green moss onto the bed of the frame, then attach lengths of bamboo or bark as the surround.

Once the glue dries, you can add all manner of decoration: acorns, mushrooms, lichen, seedpods, succulents, a pair of cobaea seedpods, a couple of stems of passion vine, and perhaps a few twigs edged in yellow lichen.

ACORN TABLE CENTERPIECE –
Two forest pieces here—one simple, one complex. Note the glass plate (*opposite, top right*): it forms the perfect frame for a collection of oak leaves. How easy is that? Instead of leaves, you can also flatten a single fern under the plate. The centerpiece begins with three circles of rough birch disks, glued together so each piece is on half the previous one—like a tiny staircase. Add whatever appeals to this base: shelf mushrooms, acorns, succulents, seedpods, and pieris branches. The tiny, green orbs are decorative muskmelons (*Cucumis*).

(*above*) A close-up of the centerpiece on the previous page, (*opposite*) this view shows the details of shelf mushrooms, acorns, succulents, seedpods, and pieris branches.

BARK BOAT - Here's a piece of bark that can carry a plethora of acorns, tillandsias, a mushroom smokestack, and magnolia buds as sails. A giant shelf mushroom anchors the champagne tray.

5.

LICHENS

Ivy, lichens and wallflowers need
ruin to make them grow.
— NATHANIEL HAWTHORNE

There's an otherworldly beauty to lichen, the strange forest denizen, which appears so prolifically in the Pacific Northwest. Although lichen looks plantlike, it is not a plant. Rather, it is the child of a symbiotic relationship between fungi and algae. The dominant partner is the fungi, but it is the algae that can convert sunlight to nourishment, helping the organism grow. Like moss, lichens are an early building block of soil. But, for me, they are "rock stars," distinctive characters in many of my arrangements.

It's not difficult to be inspired by lichen in my neck of the woods. Find an aging stand of Douglas fir, and some of its limbs will drip with witch's hair, a stringy lichen. Just as common is reindeer moss— actually, a lichen—which reminds me of tiny Popsicle trees and grows abundantly in rocky crevices. Still other lichens look like fringy, gray-green lettuces that hold their shape and snuggle comfortably into corners of a still life.

Lichen is the child of a symbiotic relationship between fungi and algae.

When I search for lichen, I look first for weathered limbs encased in greens and grays and scattered on the sidewalk from gusty winds. I carry these home in a backpack and add them to my collection of special finds. Friends are always finding small bits of lichen to add to my collection, but just like other woodland elements, those you can't find in your backyard are usually for sale at craft stores or on the internet.

If you are harvesting lichen from private land with permission, it's good to remember that these plants provide food, cover, and nesting material for many birds, so it's best to collect lightly. In its dry form, lichen is long-lasting, so I can reuse pieces of it in many different arrangements.

Lichens can help you capture the textural quality of a forest scene. Juxtapose the various types against acorns and mushrooms, glue some gray-green wisps into the corner of a still life, and suddenly the contrast of brown pinecones, green moss, red acorns, and gray lichens helps capture a moment in time.

HOW TO WORK WITH LICHEN

Scientists estimate that 6 percent of the Earth's surface is covered in lichen. This is not surprising, given that this composite organism (both algae and fungi) can adapt to a wide variety of temperatures. Lichens grow in arctic tundra, in dry deserts, along rocky coastlines, and in old-growth forests. Since lichen takes decades to grow, be careful about from where and how much you gather, even if you have permission to do so. You should gather only varieties found on broken limbs on the forest floor. Dried lichen is gray and something you might be able to find at a craft store or flower market, depending on where you live. If your lichen is more green than gray, and therefore not quite dry, spray your arrangement with water to keep it fresh.

WALKING STICK LICHENS

Branches covered in gray, gold, or white lichen add character to any arrangement. I'll often cut a branch and nestle it into a still life. But one of my favorite ways to display lichens is to gather a variety of different branches—white or yellow birch, oak, or ash—that are coated in lichen, the whole length of a walking stick, and just lean them against a wall. They are like an instant science project, drawing visitors to look and look again.

How I See . . .
LICHEN

Lichens thrive in ancient forests, since these woods provide an undisturbed environment in which they can grow. The older the forest, the more branches and bark are covered in the slow-growing miracle. Every branch I gather and save has an intricate and unique pattern of gray-green covering its length. These sticks of patterned wood form a superstructure in the woods and do the same for my still lifes. Look carefully at the textures they create; they appear as different as snowflakes.

Tips for Making
A WOODLAND WREATH

I love making these woodland wreaths and like to use elements that do not require a water source so they can be enjoyed for many months. You can use pieces of bark, interesting branches, or small pieces of wood, and display a variety of seedpods from trees, shrubs, annuals, or perennials during the fall. Also incorporate any interesting finds from the garden or flower market that will still look nice when dried.

The 16-inch wreath frames I used can be purchased at most craft stores. Using paddle wire (gauge 26), attach a moss base to the frame by winding wire around the moss every inch or so. If necessary, use cold glue to attach any straggling pieces. Then use a glue gun to attach the decoration.

This wreath contains moss, bark, lichen, dried mushrooms, a variety of seedpods (eucalyptus, *Cardiocrinum,* devil's claw, screwbean mesquite), acorns, dried ferns, pinecones, succulents, and cacti. I like to place the smaller elements before gluing them, so I can change their position if need be; I often do this in sections.

Bring It Home

BLOOMING WALL HANGING –
A metal armature lifts this crusty log into the air, making the decorative opportunities that much greater. Twigs of red fuchsia sunk into AgraWool provide height and color. Next come ferns, seedpods, and green blueberries. Chartreuse alchemilla adds fluff and contrasts with the texture of lime nicotiana. Place curly, gray leaves of *Tillandsia xerographica* (an air plant that requires no water), and drape old man's beard lichen and wood shavings on the countertop.

NATURAL VASE – Here, I used a glue gun to attach lichen-covered branches to a clay pot. Additional smaller branches emerge from a sea of green and purple hellebores and checkerboard fritillaria.

TULIP FRAME – The frame was fashioned by securing branches covered with chartreuse lichen I bought at the flower market to a wire frame. I used a glue gun to attach more lichen as well as spider plants and twigs. For color, I added orange tulips, each of which is still attached to the bulb to remain fresh.

LICHEN COMPOTE –
A picturesque log is balanced in a shallow compote that is lined with AgraWool. The base of the compote displays a contrast of greens—from chartreuse to darker shades. In addition to the variety of lichens spilling over the rim, you can add geranium leaves, jasmine and Chilean glory vines, and poppy seedpods.

CIRCLE CENTERPIECE – The intense heat of a forest fire curled this
branch into an almost perfect circle. I've wrapped the sphere in passion vine,
adding sweet peas for color. The base is decorated with lichens, clematis,
sweet peas, brodiaea, alchemilla, hellebore, ferns, and blueberries.

ORCHID FRAME – This orchid frame looks elaborate, but it is simple to make. Use hot glue to attach gray lichen to the base of the tray. Choose a gnarled piece of wood. The moth orchids were purchased at the supermarket and tucked into water tubes that are hidden by the wood or lichen. I left the orchids on the top in the 2-inch pots. With lots of care and some luck, they will rebloom in a few months.

LICHEN WREATH – Like the seedpod wreath on page 180, this construction starts with a wire-wreath frame. Zip-tie branches covered with chartreuse lichen to the frame, and add tiny succulents and a collection of acorns and pinecones. In the Pacific Northwest, a wreath like this will be watered by regular rain and moisture in the air.

RASPBERRY CENTERPIECE - A wayward piece
of dried seaweed circles a "bird's nest" of green lichen.
Unripe blueberries and a handful of red raspberries
join a two-tone succulent at the table.

SEAWEED CHANDELIER – *(opposite)*
The structure for this pinecone chandelier are the branches woven together to form an organic rounded shape. In addition to the pinecones hanging down, there are strips of dried seaweed and pieces of lichen tucked between the branches to create lots of texture and visual interest.

6.

FERNS

---

*It is through ferns that one can
describe the essence of shade.*
— FOERSTER

When I was a child, I thought of ferns as "fairy fans"—triangles of tiny leaves that skirted the bouquets I would gather for my mother. On woodland walks, they were a familiar sight, emerging from craggy rocks or carpeting the forest floor. My sister and I would pick handfuls of these gentle swords, sometimes stripping the leaves like confetti as we hiked. Other times, we'd wonder at the symmetrical spores that appeared like candy dots on the backs of the fronds. In spring, we delighted in watching new growth sprout as tightly curled fiddleheads slowly unfurled to catch the light.

Only later, as an adult, did I understand that ferns were prehistoric plants, dating back more than 400 million years. Those tiny spores were an early form of reproduction that has kept these plants multiplying abundantly in tropical and temperate forests. Today, ferns are a constant in my botanical arrangements. Together with moss and lichen, they reflect the soul of a healthy forest.

Damp weather in the Pacific Northwest encourages an abundance of fern varieties. In the spring, I'll buy young ostrich or lady ferns and tack them up on a wall for decoration. Without water, they will curl in on themselves in a day, but even as they dry, they embody a forest moment. When setting a table, try placing a fern frond underneath a clear, glass plate as decoration. Sometimes, I preserve ferns by pressing them to dry in an old atlas (see page 214). Once flattened, they can be displayed in picture frames.

There are lady, oak, and sword ferns in our woods, but my favorite is the western maidenhair fern. Its wispy leaves fan out like tiny umbrellas held on a sturdy stalk. I only look to the forest for inspiration, but I don't pick ferns from the forest floor. I use only ferns I grow or from plants I buy at flower markets and garden centers. Many garden centers sell dozens of varieties. I grow these in my shade garden, often snipping fronds as I build an arrangement. They are particularly valuable when an oversize leaf needs some softening. The fern's fine-textured foliage will add just the right contrast.

Whenever I use ferns in an arrangement, a water source is required, since these are plants that thrive in damp forests. When branches are anchored in AgraWool that is hidden by lichen or moss, the leaves stay open and bright for three to four days. If you want to keep the arrangement longer, just remove the ferns, or replace them.

You can shop for a variety of tropical ferns at your local garden center. I keep multiple pots in my studio, clipping fronds as I need them. Take, for example, the bird's nest fern, a common houseplant that is identified by its flat, wavy, or crinkly fronds. It reminds me of a seaweed plant growing on dry land. Again, it is the special texture of the leaves that makes these ferns so useful in my work. When tucked into an arrangement, they echo a sense of place—deep woods and ferns undulating in an afternoon breeze.

Ferns reflect the soul
of a healthy forest.

How I See...
FERNS

Ferns are a good problem-solving plant
in a forest landscape. They halt erosion
and cover bare ground efficiently. They
are particularly good at climbing hills,
cascading over one another in a sea of
waving fronds. The forests of the Pacific
Northwest teem with ferns—sword,
ostrich, and maidenhair—this last my
favorite for its sheer delicacy. When
walking in the woods, I'll spy a fern
growing out of a rock face or the crotch
of a tree. How does it get there, I
wonder? I'll reproduce that serendipity in
my arrangements.

PRESSED FERNS AND FLOWERS

Preserving the botanical moment by pressing ferns, leaves, and flowers at their peak is an art form that goes back to the ancient Egyptians. Because they are sturdy and so "architectural," ferns are excellent candidates for pressing. Gather fresh ferns and remove any curled or dying leaves. Put each fern between paper towels and place it in a heavy book (I use an old atlas). Leave it to dry for a week or two. The flattened leaves can then be framed and hung on the wall or used as decoration lying flat on a table. I sometimes place the ferns on a dinner napkin or under a clear, glass dinner plate to display them.

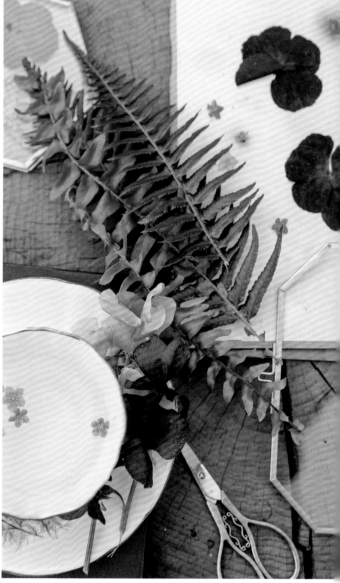

How to Make
A WOODLAND ARRANGEMENT

I've assembled these woodland displays for weddings or other special events, and they always draw an appreciative crowd. Their look depends on how you assemble the wood pieces: some will be wide and broad; others, like this one (*opposite*), will reach higher. I like using one botanical element to visually connect the logs; in this case, I used a pink jasmine vine. You might also use ivy or any vine that's growing in your garden.

I first assembled the wood pieces, drilling holes in the horizontal and vertical bark. They were attached using zip ties, but you can also screw them together. I didn't want to obscure the wood structure in this piece, since it was so

reminiscent of a forest moment. Instead, I glued elements onto the top, center, and base, making sure to wind the jasmine vine throughout. Every arrangement like this depends on the materials you assemble. No two will be alike, which adds to their charm.

I used pink jasmine vine, dried mushrooms, seedpods, pussy willow, succulents, dried fiddlehead ferns, pinecones, moss, and various lichens. Place the jasmine vine (or another leggy vine) into a water tube and set the tube behind a log so it is hidden. Cold-glue on moss and lichens, followed by other elements. Spray with water every other week to keep succulents happy. You can add water to the tube or replace the jasmine when it wilts.

Bring It Home

SIDE TABLE ARRANGEMENT ⤙⤙ 223

WOODSY COMPOTE ⤙⤙ 224

FOREST VASES ⤙⤙ 227

SIDE TABLE ARRANGEMENT – Anything can be a container. In
this case, I attached a craggy piece of wood as the base. Hide a piece
of AgraWool in the wooden hollow and add a contrasting collection
of ferns. Finish with a wraparound of dried grapevine.

WOODSY COMPOTE – This arrangement
of ferns, branches, allium, fiddleheads,
succulents, tillandsias, and date palm shoots is
held by a glass compote covered in birch bark.

FOREST VASES – I purchased these bits of birch log at the Portland Flower Market. They came with a water tube "vase" that is perfect for holding a single blossom or, in this case, a wavy fern. Individual vases holding a variety of ferns make an easy table setting. Decorate napkins with stones and more ferns to echo the forest setting.

Appendix

NOTES ON FORAGING

I love walking in the woods and finding special bits of flora I can bring home and use in my rustic creations. But I am careful where I go and careful about what I harvest. Having read this book, you know that most of my collecting is confined to the natural refuse found on the forest floor and collected with permission from private land. It's the rare landowner who will complain if you collect windblown limbs or gather acorns in the wild. But as I've said before, you must ask permission, even for such simple items.

I am fortunate to have friends who invite me to forage carefully in their woods, but sometimes it's not even necessary to leave home. I find numerous downed limbs and pretty seedpods in my own Portland neighborhood. Especially in the fall, a brisk morning walk has me gathering all sorts of windblown ephemera.

To forage farther afield, you'll have to do some research. The United States is home to 400 national parks, 560 national wildlife refuges, and over 250 million acres of other public lands, and each one has its own rules about foraging. Most of our major national parks, like Yosemite or Yellowstone, do not allow foraging. However, some national forests do allow visitors to collect edible or decorative materials if they apply for a permit.

The best way to find out about foraging on public lands in your state is to go to www.fs.usda.gov. Once on this site, which lists every public forest in the country, you can search by state; within each state, you can find a link to any public forest. Once you've selected a forest, look for a quick link to "Passes & Permits." Under that heading you will find information on permits for the "Collection of Forest Products."

Even within the same state, the rules differ from one forest to another. These rules often change from year to year, depending on weather, fire risk, and other variables, so it's best to check with the district office before you set off.

For me, a favorite source for unusual forest products is the Portland Flower Market, which has several vendors who have permits to forage in the state parks. I've found many special pieces at the flower market, including a rock with a stump growing around it.

Most major cities have a wholesale flower market, although some can be difficult to visit if you don't have a business tax ID. That said, some allow visitors if they pay an entrance fee, and many will welcome shoppers after their wholesale customers have left for the day. These markets

Statistics from: https://www.doi.gov/blog/americas-public-lands-explained
https://www.fs.usda.gov/main/crgnsa/passes-permits

open as early as 5 a.m., which is when the regulars shop, but if you visit later, after 8:30 in the morning, you can usually find vendors who will sell to you.

You can also shop on the internet. Google any item mentioned in this book, and you can find an online source. Search "Burr Acorns," for example, and you'll find a handful of sites that can sell you these or a dozen other varieties. It's wonderful to have the World Wide Web as a resource, but I don't recommend using it with

any frequency. By the time you pay for your product and the shipping, you will find the costs prohibitive. If you want an acorn, it's better to search for it in your own backyard.

One thing you might consider buying online is sheet moss. If I'm teaching a workshop, I often order moss delivered directly to my classroom. If you are making a single still life that requires moss for the base, using storebought moss will evoke the feeling of a wild forest floor without impacting the natural beauty that inspired you.

KNOW YOUR SPECIES

It's helpful to be able to identify the various species you come across in the woods. First, it's good to know whether you are dealing with invasive or threatened species (pick all you want of the former; respect the latter). Second, part of the pleasure in doing this work is learning more about the various ferns, nuts, mushrooms,

mosses, and lichens you are gathering. A good field guide will give you tips on the soil and weather conditions that promote growth and point you in the right direction. The same is true for a field guide to trees and shrubs. The more you learn about native habitats, the more you will appreciate and feel comfortable in them.

FIELD GUIDES

Here are some recommendations:

The Peterson Field Guide to Trees and Shrubs. Be sure to purchase the correct region, as there are different field guides for each part of the United States.

The National Geographic Pocket Guide to Trees and Shrubs of North America is smaller than Perterson's and more user-friendly. Since it's pocket-sized and covers the entire country, it's

not as comprehensive, but it has all the most common species and is good for the beginning botanist.

The National Audubon Society Field Guide to Flowers and *The Peterson Field Guide to Wildflowers* are both good primers. If you live in the Pacific Northwest, as I do, another favorite reference is *Plants of Coastal British Columbia Including Washington, Oregon & Alaska* by Jim Pojar and Andy MacKinnon.

FORAGING GUIDES

Most books about foraging focus more on edible plants than on beguiling flora you might harvest for a decorative arrangement. That said, some are very good at teaching you how to see plants that you would otherwise ignore. You can also find out more about mushrooms in your region and learn where to hunt for berries.

Pacific Northwest Edible Plant Foraging: A Field Guide to Find, Identify, Harvest and Prepare Wild Edibles by Norman Owen.

Timber Press publishes a series of seven guides that cover foraging in all regions of the United States: *Midwest Foraging, Southwest Foraging, Southeast Foraging, Northeast Foraging, Pacific Northwest Foraging, California Foraging,* and *Mountain States Foraging.*

SHOP LOCAL

As mentioned earlier, I frequently wander no farther than my local supermarket for all sorts of treasures, from fruits and vegetables to dried flowers, potted plants, and seasonal bulbs. Most local craft shops carry wire-wreath forms, wooden frames, and other useful tools.

A well-stocked garden center will have a selection of succulents, begonias, tiny orchids, and other flora to add to your arrangements. I always, for example, keep a half-dozen fern varieties on hand.

RESOURCES

GARDENING TOOLS

Your local garden center, Home Depot, Amazon

HAND DRILLS AND DRILL BITS

Your local hardware store, Home Depot, Lowe's

GLUES

Your local art supply store, Michaels, Amazon

OASIS FLORAL ADHESIVE

Your local florist, Michaels, Amazon

ROUND AND SQUARE WREATH FRAMES

Your local garden center, Michaels, Home Depot, Amazon

WOODEN FRAMES WITH CANVAS BACKING (USED FOR FRAMED WOODLAND MONTAGES)

Your local art supply store, Michaels, Amazon

MOSS

Your local florist or garden center, Michaels, Amazon

WOODEN DISKS

Your local art supply store, Michaels, Home Depot, Amazon

LIST OF INGREDIENTS

When I began making woodland arrangements, my early creations were built from materials gathered nearby and from my own backyard garden. As my business has grown, so has my geography. When I travel to other parts of the country to give workshops, I often return home with forest treasures I've been given by my students or found on my own. Some former students even send boxes of sustainably foraged materials that they gather for me. We're like a club, trading cherished finds among friends.

All the dried plant material I collect goes into deep baskets that I rummage through when I'm creating a still life. The living plants line my workshop's shelves, where I can clip leaves or blossoms to add color and movement.

Listed below are the materials I use most frequently, but anything you gather can be added to the mix.

Alchemilla (lady's mantle)

Asclepia (butterfly weed)

Bark

Berries: unripe blueberries, raspberries, and blackberries; viburnum berries

Brodiaea (cluster lillies)

Cacti

Eccremocarpus (Chilean glory flower)

Ferns: my favorites are maidenhair and bird's nest

Foliage of cotinus (smoke bush), geranium, calathea

Fritillaria

Fuchsia

Hellebore

Lichens

Moth orchids

Mushrooms

Nicotiana (tobacco plants)

Penstemon (beardtonuges)

Pinecones

River rocks

Rose hips

Seaweed (dried)

Sedum

Seedpods: abutilon, alstroemeria, angelica, beech, cardiocrinum, columbine, datura, devil's claws, eucalyptus, honey locust, lilies, lupine, nigella, oak (acorns), peonies, poppies, screwbean mesquite, wisteria

Spider plant

Succulents: string of pearls, rhipsalis, ceropegia

Sweet peas

Tendrils of sweet peas, passion vine, and grapevine

Tillandsia xerographica

Vines: clematis, hops, jasmine, passion vine

Wood shavings

Acknowledgments

In the fall of 2020, Leslie Jonath, who is now my agent, contacted me on Instagram, asking if I was writing a book. My answer was No, but I would like to talk with you. And so began this journey.

My deepest appreciation goes to the many who made this book possible. Writing a book takes a village, and I could not have asked for a better team:

Theresa Bear, who not only took the exquisite photos but also spent endless hours finding the perfect locations and directed the photo shoots impeccably. Your creative energy is magical.

Jen Rich and Gwen Severson, who helped brainstorm the details of every shoot and styled each one perfectly.

Julie Michaels, who instinctively understood my love of Nature and wrote the stories and descriptions so eloquently for each chapter.

Leslie Jonath, who has been so helpful and supportive throughout the process and who connected all the dots so well.

And the team at Clarkson Potter Publishing, especially to editor Deanne Katz for her thoughtful guidance and stewardship, and to Mia Johnson for her beautiful designs.

A heartfelt thank-you to so many friends for their unfailing support and to those who gathered and foraged special seedpods and other textures for many of the designs in this book, in particular: Elizabeth Bryant, Kate Bryant, Linda Barclay, Deborah Meyers, Catalina Garreton, Lalena Dolby, Heather Dillon, Annette Gomez, Sheryl Tynes, Nancy Cutler, Morgan Moylan, Amy McGee, Tamara Gibson, Tiffany Garner, and Andre Burgogne. And many thanks to the owners of Wilson Farm.

Library of Congress Cataloging-in-Publication Data

Names: Weeks, Françoise, author. Title: Wonder of the woodlands / Françoise Weeks with Theresa Bear ; photographs by Theresa Bear. Identifiers: LCCN 2023016300 (print) | LCCN 2023016301 (ebook) | ISBN 9780593578384 (hardcover) | ISBN 9780593578391 (ebook) Subjects: LCSH: Floral decorations. | Botanical specimens in interior decoration. | Flower arrangement in interior decoration. Classification: LCC SB449 .W395 2024 (print) | LCC SB449 (ebook) | DDC 745.92—dc23/eng/20230825
LC record available at https://lccn.loc.gov/2023016300
LC ebook record available at https://lccn.loc.gov/2023016301

ISBN 978-0-593-57838-4
Ebook ISBN 978-0-593-57839-1

Printed in China

Written by Françoise Weeks with Julie Michaels
Editor: Deanne Katz
Designer: Mia Johnson
Production editor: Patricia Shaw
Production manager: Jessica Heim
Compositors: Merri Ann Morrell and Zoe Tokushige
Prop stylist: Jen Rich
Prop stylist assistant: Gwen Severson
Copyeditor: Diana Drew
Proofreader: Kathy Brock
Marketer: Allison Renzulli

10 9 8 7 6 5 4 3 2 1

First Edition